ZOO CLUES 2

My Teeth Are Sharp and Pointy

by Jessica Rudolph

Consultant:
Christopher Kuhar, PhD
Executive Director
Cleveland Metroparks Zoo
Cleveland, Ohio

BEARPORT PUBLISHING

New York, New York

Credits
Cover, © Doug Perrine/Minden Pictures; 4–5, © Peter Atkinson/Alamy Stock Photo; 6–7, © Frank Lane/Minden Pictures; 8–9, © Amilevin/Dreamstime; 10–11, © Doug Perrine/Seapics; 12–13, © Doug Perrine/Minden Pictures; 14–15, © Doug Perrine/Minden Pictures; 16–17, © Doug Perrine/Minden Pictures; 18–19, © blickwinkel/Alamy Stock Photo and © Vilainecrevette/Shutterstock; 20–21, © blickwinkel/Alamy Stock Photo and © Vilainecrevette/Shutterstock; 22, © Tempestz/Dreamstime; 23, © Charline Tetiyevsky/Dreamstime; 24, © stephanie phillips/iStock.

Publisher: Kenn Goin
Editor: J. Clark
Creative Director: Spencer Brinker
Design: Debrah Kaiser

Library of Congress Cataloging-in-Publication Data

Names: Rudolph, Jessica, author.
Title: My teeth are sharp and pointy / by Jessica Rudolph.
Description: New York, New York : Bearport Publishing, [2017] | Series: Zoo clues 2 | Audience: Ages 6–9._ | Includes bibliographical references and index.
Identifiers: LCCN 2016007670 (print) | LCCN 2016011670 (ebook) | ISBN 9781944102562 (library binding) | ISBN 9781944102951 (ebook)
Subjects: LCSH: Sawfishes—Juvenile literature.
Classification: LCC QL638.77 R83 2017 (print) | LCC QL638.77 (ebook) | DDC 597.3/5—dc23
LC record available at http://lccn.loc.gov/2016007670

For more information, write to Bearport Publishing Company, Inc., 45 West 21st Street, Suite 3B, New York, New York 10010. Printed in the United States of America.

10 9 8 7 6 5 4 3 2 1

Contents

What Am I?

Look at my fins.

They are thin
and gray.

My skin
feels rough.

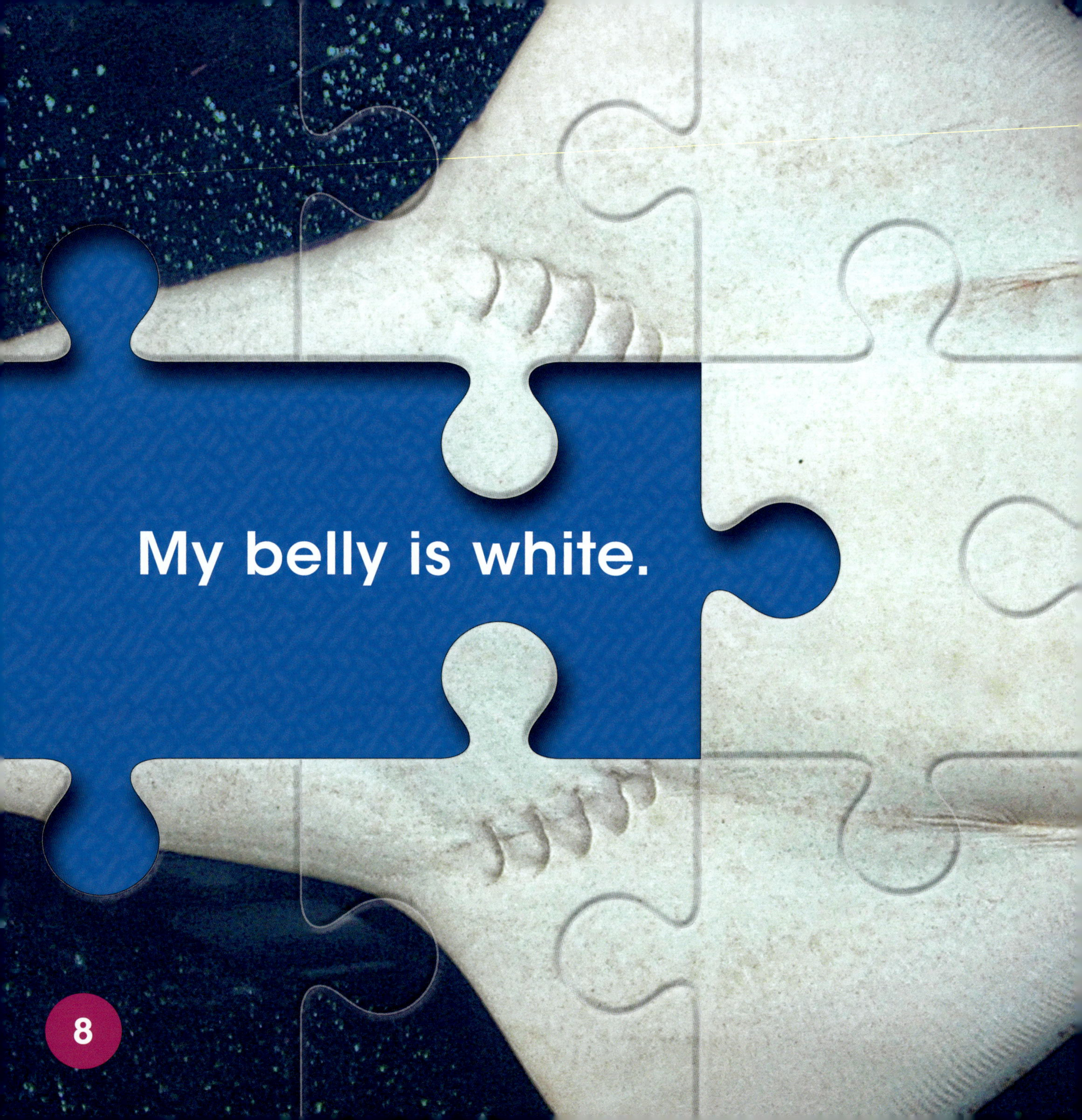

My belly is white.

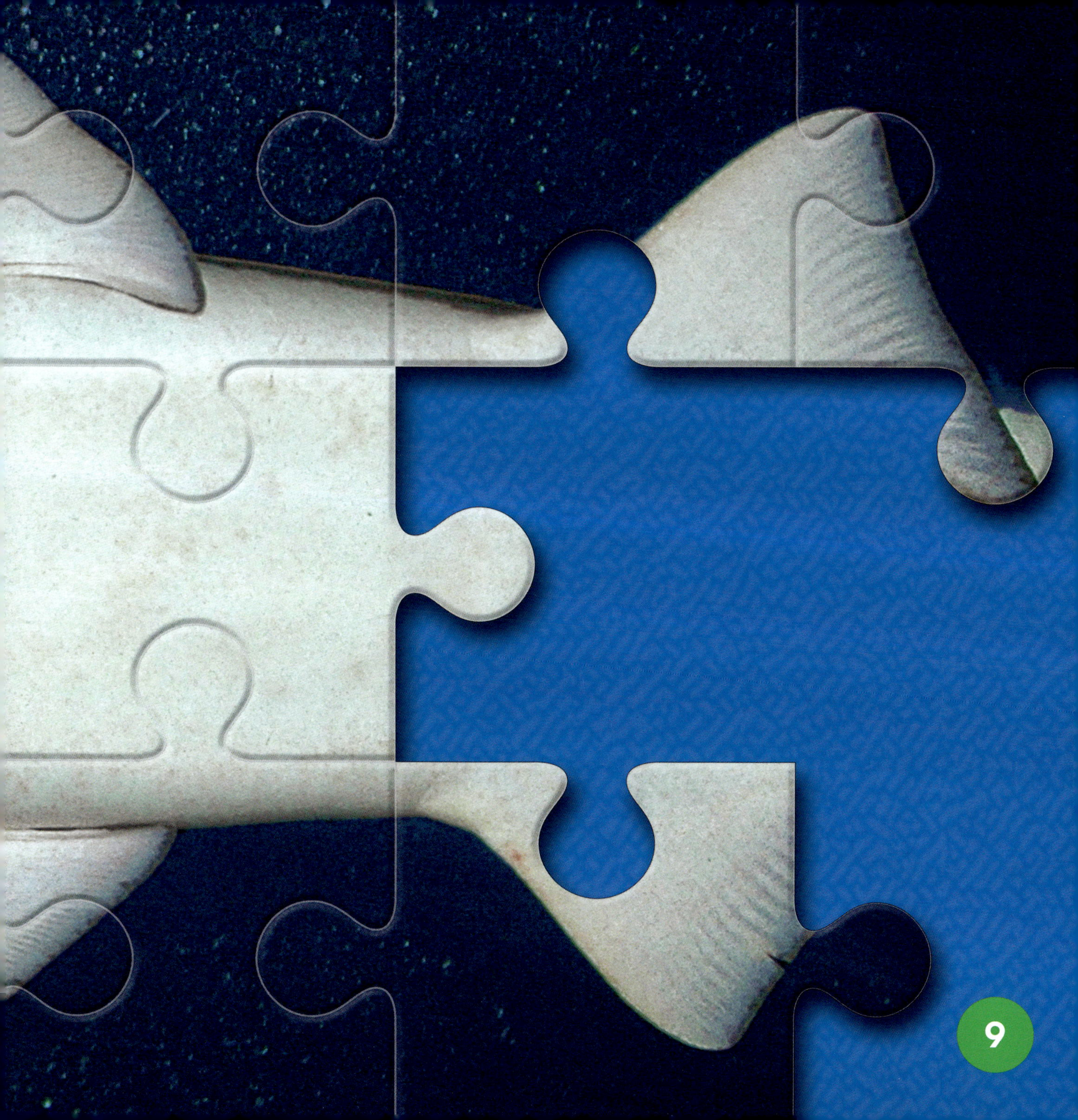

I have a strong tail.

It helps me swim.

My snout is flat.

It is very
long, too.

My teeth are sharp and pointy.

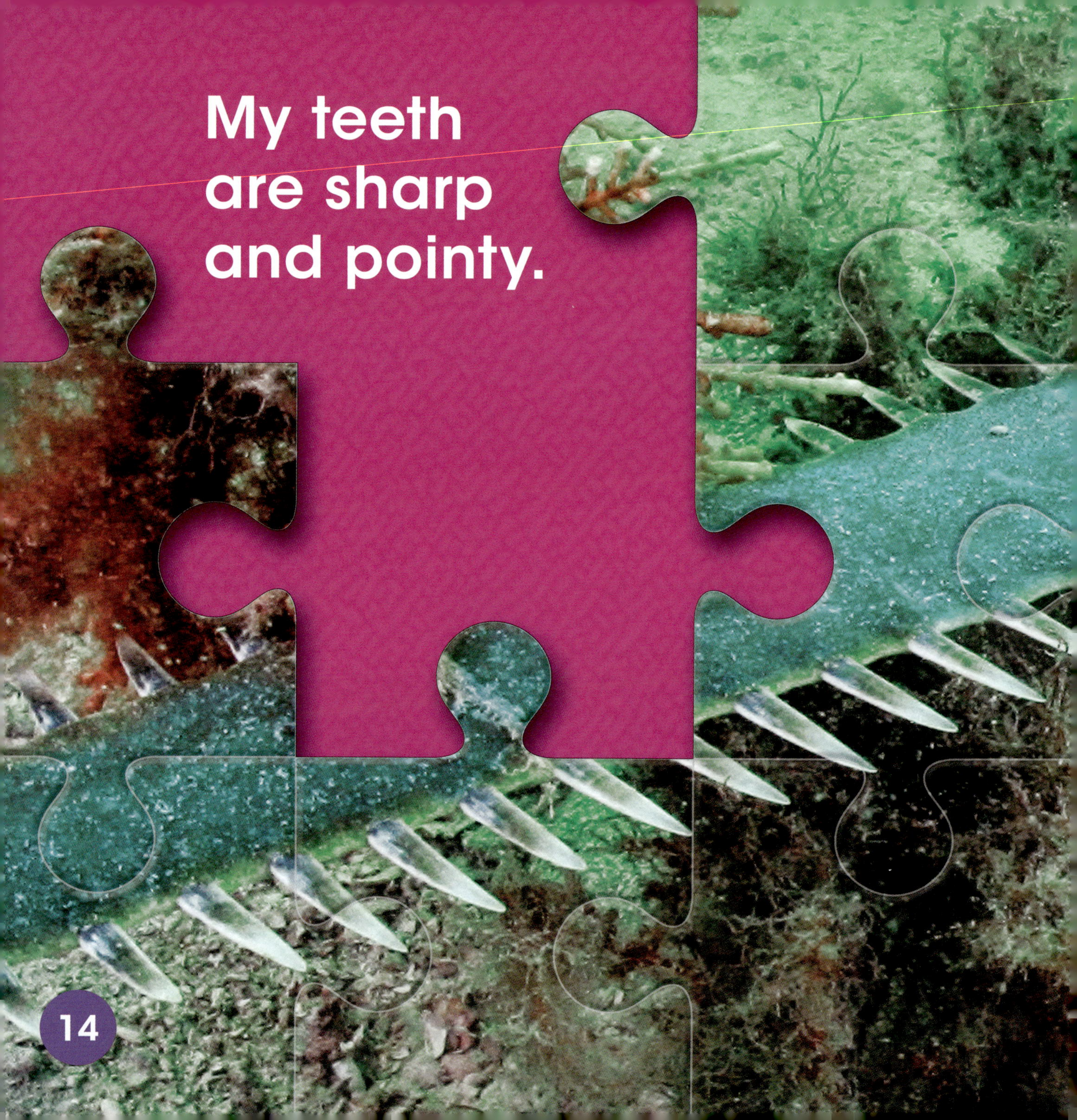

They stick out
of my snout.

I have two round eyes.

They are yellow and black.

What am I?

Let's find out!

I am a sawfish!

Animal Facts

Sawfish are related to rays and sharks. Like all fish, they use gills to breathe. Unlike most fish, they give birth to live young instead of laying eggs.

More Sawfish Facts

Food:	Small fish, crabs, lobsters, and shrimps
Size:	Up to 23 feet (7 m) long
Weight:	About 1,000 pounds (454 kg)
Life Span:	Around 30 years in the wild
Cool Fact:	A sawfish can attack small fish by quickly shaking its snout from side to side. The animals get caught on the sawfish's sharp teeth.

Where Do I Live?

Sawfish live in oceans and rivers in many parts of the world.

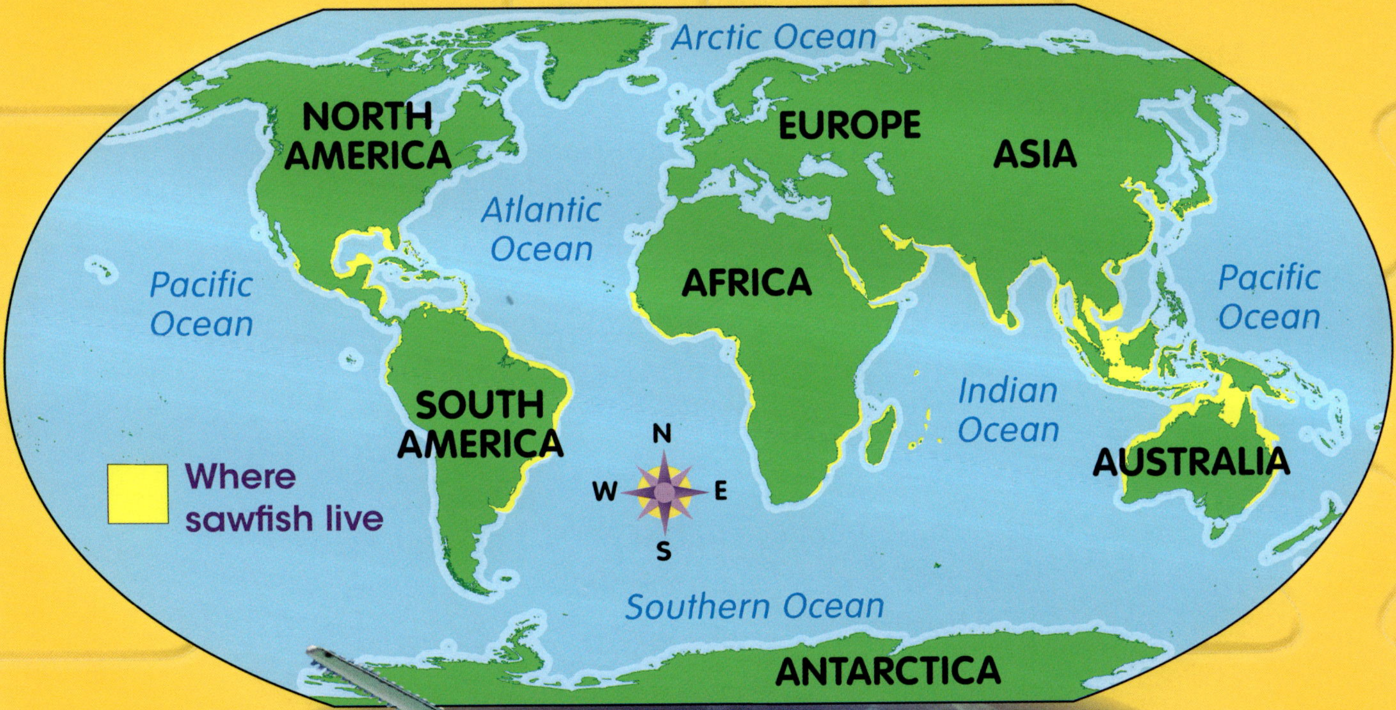

Index

Read More

MacQuitty, Miranda. *Shark (DK Eyewitness Books).* New York: Dorling Kindersley (2014).

Walker, Sally M. *Rays (Nature Watch).* Minneapolis, MN: Carolrhoda Books (2003).

Learn More Online

To learn more about sawfish, visit
www.bearportpublishing.com/ZooClues

About the Author

Jessica Rudolph lives in Connecticut. She has edited and written many books about history, science, and nature for children.

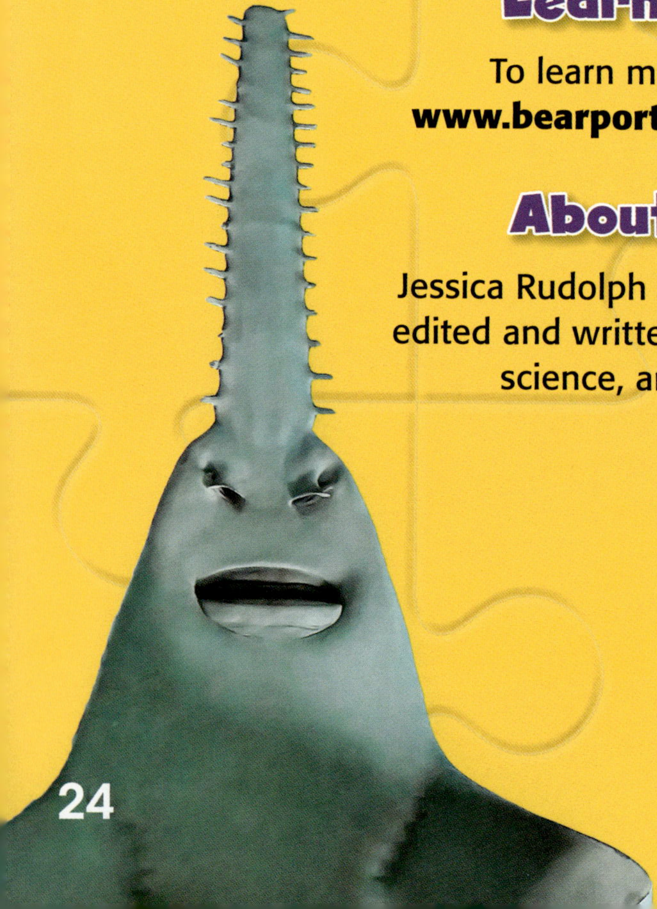